Library of Congress Control Number: 2025914286

ISBN: 979-8-9986488-1-6

Copyright
2025 by Heather Denton
All right reserved. No part of this publication may be reproduced, distributed, or transmitted in any form or by any means,
or stored in a database or retrieval system, without the prior written permission of the of the
copyright holder, except by a reviewer who may quote brief passages in a review.

Dedication:

For all my fellow humans who are looking for a better, more simple way of life.

Thank you to my husband who finally came around to my way of thinking.

WYOMING

From an East Coast Perspective

Written and Photographed by:
Heather Denton

Imagine living your whole life in the same place. 44 years to be exact. And then one day, you tell your husband that you want to move west to live a simpler life. Then, a year or so later, you are packing up your house, your dog, and your cat, and you're moving 2000 miles west to a place you have never even visited. That's what my husband and I did.

I was born and raised in Fall River, MA. I traveled throughout the world, and some of my own country, but this was huge.

This book is not about great photographs; this is a book about experiences, told through pictures.

I'll try not to bore you with too many pictures of my husband and I, but sometimes they are necessary.

The Beginning

"Go confidently in the direction of your dreams. Live the life you have imagined."
Henry David Thoreau

Whose idea was this anyway? The truck is packed, the house is empty and under contract but has not closed yet, we are essentially homeless, and we are heading west in the middle of a Nor'easter. Perfect.

Hugo, our dog, is not thrilled, we're a bit squished, and it's snowing. Oh, and we're moving to a city we've never been to, in a state we know nothing about. On the bright side, the cat is perfectly content.

The pets were comfy during the whole 3-day journey. Maybe not hotel-bed-all-day kind of comfy, but we did the best we could.

Basically, our view for 3 days. Thankfully, our journey was uneventful.

FINALLY!

"Are those the Tetons?" Craig and I wondered. No, they are not. When I say that we know nothing about Wyoming, I am being mostly literal. We know about Yellowstone National Park and Grand Teton National Park, and we know that we will not be living very close to either of those places. But we had zero idea how vast Wyoming is.

Our new home city! I've learned that people do not like for Casper to be called a city, but it is classified as a city. I say call it whatever you like. We're calling it home.

The Scenery

Imagine this is your daily commute?

In Massachusetts, you can go down Rte. 24 from Fall River, MA to Taunton, MA in 20 minutes...on the weekend. If you need to get to work on a weekday, there is inevitably a car accident, and now your commute is 60 minutes. That is not unusual.

Craig's commute is 12 minutes...every time. And the view on the way to work never gets old.

We were, and still are, in awe of this view. One of the first things I noticed was how much closer the clouds feel, and this picture illustrates that perfectly.

The first time we drove around Casper, we could not believe it. Getting around was a challenge at first, but it was not because of the traffic; we just didn't know where we were going. The traffic was a dream. Some days, in Fall River, MA, a 10 or 15 minute journey to the other side of the city can take an hour.

When people on the local social media groups complain about the traffic in Casper, I just chuckle.

I had to include a photo of Indian Paintbrush, Wyoming's state flower. After living here for a few years, I've come to realize it's nothing like the daffodils that pop up effortlessly along the roads in Massachusetts and Rhode Island. In the dry, rugged landscape out here, anything in bloom feels like a small miracle, and this one truly steals the show.

The Great Plains Prickly Pear is no less spectacular, but I will say that I never had to worry about being impaled when I hiked in New England.

The Scenery Part II

Road Trips

Fremont Canyon, Casper, WY

I've been to the Corinth Canal in Greece, but to me, this was just as beautiful.

This wasn't technically a road trip; it's about 45 minutes outside the city, but I am going to class it as such. Since moving here, my definition of road trip has definitely changed.

Ayres Natural Bridge, Douglas, WY

Something else that is only about 40 minutes outside of Casper is Ayres Natural Bridge. No pets allowed, which we think is a good thing. It's incredibly peaceful.

Mud swallows. I was fascinated the first time I saw them. Just one of the little things that those who are born and raised in this area take for granted, I would imagine.

Ayres Natural Bridge, Douglas, WY

 I'm not saying that there is nothing as beautiful as this in Massachusetts, I'm just saying I have never experienced this kind of peace while trying to enjoy nature. Because put this in Massachusetts, and it will be overrun with people drinking their iced coffees and having conversations that could be heard from the moon.

Devil's Tower National Monument, Devil's Tower, WY

  How do you describe Devil's Tower to someone with adequate words? I have never experienced anything like this, my own brain is struggling to comprehend, never mind trying to articulate its magnificence to someone else.

I've seen Stonehenge, the Acropolis, and I've traveled around India; I still cannot compare Devil's Tower to anything else.

Oregon Trail Ruts, Guernsey, WY

I can't say I remember learning much about the pioneers' journey west, but seeing the wagon ruts in person feels profound. Growing up on the East Coast, that part of American history felt like a distant past, but living in Wyoming, it doesn't feel so far away.

Hot Springs State Park, Thermopolis, WY

Growing up, I can't say that I thought much about hot springs. But as an adult, the only hot springs I ever heard of were the hot springs at Yellowstone National Park, but they might as well have been as far away as the Caldeiras in Portugal. So imagine my surprise when I moved to a landlocked state and heard about Hot Springs State Park.

Hot Springs State Park, Thermopolis, WY

You can have a nice soak in the hot springs (just not this one pictured) if you want to. I did. And it was like soaking in rotten egg-scented hot dog water. Would I do it again? Probably! #YOLO

Mt. Rushmore National Monument, South Dakota

I had only ever seen Mt. Rushmore on TV and in books until I moved out here. Now we've been there at least 3 times. It's a powerful experience. And I don't take it for granted. (I know it's not in Wyoming, but living in Wyoming has afforded me the opportunity to visit Mt. Rushmore.)

Yellowstone National Park, East Entrance

This is a terrible picture, but it captures one of the most momentous days of my life. Growing up, I don't remember going on any family vacations, and Yellowstone National Park feels like the epitome of the classic American family trip.

Yes, we went to New Hampshire for the day once as a family, and occasionally we would drive to the Cape for the day so my dad could go fishing, but we never had a family vacation. So this day meant a lot to me.

Yellowstone National Park, WY

Again, how do you describe this to someone? Pictures don't do it justice at all. Part of living in Wyoming that I never experienced in Massachusetts is living in nature, not just occasionally visiting it.

And that is a big part of what was missing in my life. One can't help but be consumed by the hustle and bustle when living in Massachusetts. Here in Wyoming, being intentional about being in nature feels natural and normal.

More hot springs. Who knew? Not me. Of course, I had heard of Old Faithful, but it felt distant and unreal. Like something from a postcard.

Rocky Mountain National Park, CO

Again, who knew?? I don't know if I've ever heard of RMNP before moving to this part of the country. Maybe I had. I certainly had heard about the Rocky Mountains, but it was more like something from a movie, not a place that I would actually visit.

Rocky Mountain National Park, CO

The way that the sky changed within minutes was magical. If I had taken time-lapse photos, each one would have looked like a different point of view within the park, even though I wouldn't have moved. This was also my first time experiencing altitude sickness, which I didn't even know was a "thing". You live and you learn, sometimes the hard way.

Grand Teton National Park, WY

THESE are the Tetons. We have some beautiful mountains on the East Coast, but nothing compares. Especially this viewpoint when driving towards them. It's just incredible. It makes one feel incredibly small. Being in their presence is humbling.

Grand Teton National Park, WY

I, Heather Denton, took this picture. Me. I was there. I am incredibly humbled, and I thank God every day.

Badlands National Park, SD

I know it's not Wyoming, but just like Mt. Rushmore, I could not leave it out since we can drive there in a reasonable amount of time.

Badlands National Park, SD

Sometimes I look at my pictures and wonder if it was all a dream. I feel so fortunate, more than that word can say. Growing up in Fall River, I never imagined living this life. I've traveled a bit on mission trips and visited England with my husband, but I always dreamed of road-tripping across the U.S. just for fun. No plans, just exploring at my own pace, not rushing through a schedule.

There's nothing wrong with going on mission trips to share the Gospel. I'm really grateful for those opportunities. But this was something completely different. Feeling tiny in the vastness of God's creation, seeing things my mind could barely wrap around, things I had no frame of reference for. And having the freedom to explore however I wanted is something special. Plus, I get to do silly things like hiking up a ladder and pulling a leg muscle because I forget I'm out of shape and middle-aged.

Badlands National Park, SD

I have a lot of pictures of Badlands National Park. I've been there 3 times. That's how incredible this place is.

I can't wait to go back. But there is so much more of the western part of the US to explore, so the next trip to the Badlands will have to wait.

The Wildlife

Being around animals, whether working with them or hunting them, is just part of life in Wyoming. People who grow up here might not understand why it feels like such a big deal, and that's the point of this book. My love for animals started back at Bristol County Agricultural High School in Dighton, MA, where I was surrounded by farm animals every day.

Someone once told my husband and me that some visitors to Yellowstone have never even been in nature, and that stuck with me. I had been lucky enough to experience the outdoors back East. I saw moose in Maine, deer in New Hampshire and Massachusetts, and spent time in nature throughout my life. But seeing wildlife every day is something entirely different. It makes me sad to think there are people who have never experienced that. Nature teaches you a lot about yourself, and missing out on that means missing something important.

When I was formatting this book, I put all the pictures in first, then I went back to add these little captions. I could not wait to get to this part. I saved the best for last.

Bull elk in Yellowstone National Park.

Cow elk.

A mouse at Boysen State Park, WY

Not sure what type, but I saw this owl at Custer State Park, SD

I LOVE magpies. My husband says that I am like a magpie because I love shiny things. I also have a tattoo of a magpie.
I had NO IDEA that magpies existed in the United States of America!

The only time I ever saw a magpie was in England. I never saw them in Massachusetts. They don't live in Massachusetts. Imagine my surprise when I started seeing them when I moved to Wyoming. I was delighted. And now I take lots of pictures of them.

According to a quick web browser search, magpies are part of the corvid family, along with ravens and crows. They are known for being highly intelligent, which probably explains why I like them so much

My husband and I call these "old faithfuls", because no matter where you go in Wyoming, you will see them. This is the pronghorn antelope. The 2nd fastest land mammal in the world.

I heard about them from the old song, "where the deer and the antelope play",* but I had no idea what they were. I never saw one in my life, not even at a zoo. Now I see them literally everywhere I go, and I love it.

My husband and I decided to go for a ride one sunny weekend afternoon. As we were driving, we saw a pronghorn with its leg stuck in a barbed wire fence. Fully understanding that sometimes these things happen, my husband could not just drive past. He stopped the car, safely crossed the road, and helped this poor pronghorn, who miraculously was not hurt or bleeding. That never happened in Massachusetts, or my husband's home country of England. Another incredible experience.

*" Home on the Range" was written by Dr. Brewster M. Higley in 1870, according to Wikipedia.

According to the National Park Service, the North American Bison is the largest land mammal in North America. And although people in Wyoming love to argue about what they're called, buffalo vs. bison, the scientific name is *bison bison bison*, which covers genus, species, and subspecies. So I'll continue to call them bison and upset a lot of people, but I will know in my heart that I'm right.

The only bison I had ever seen in my life, up until this point, was the sad, lonely bison at Buttonwood Park Zoo in New Bedford, MA. But I have since learned that the males are solitary creatures, because the herd is matriarchal. They kick the boys out once they've mated. So maybe that singular bison wasn't lonely at all, but rather he was living his life in peace, with no paternal responsibilities.

These creatures are truly magnificent, and these photos were taken from the safety of my vehicle. Please don't ever walk up on them. We were driving through Hot Springs State Park, and they were on the road; we knew better than to approach them. Even though I had never experienced this in my life, my self-preservation instincts kicked in. I'm not sure why other people choose not to listen to that little voice.

It's very difficult to resist petting these cute babies, but DON'T DO IT! These mamas are fierce. My husband and I were driving through Custer State Park in South Dakota, and the cows were walking on the road with their babies. One of the cows looked me right in the eyeball, and my heart started beating faster even though I knew there was a barrier. As majestic as these creatures were, once again, my instincts told me not to mess with them. Even if they started it.

Another poor quality photo, but I NEVER KNEW BADGERS EXISTED IN THE U.S. OF A.! I don't know how to articulate that. My husband has no idea how I spotted this little creature; it was pretty far away, and I made him stop the car so I could get a photo. I was dancing in my seat. A BADGER! Who would have thought? Every Wyomingite, but not me.

All my Fall River peeps, does anyone remember the Buttonwood Park Zoo (New Bedford, MA) prairie dog habitat with the domes? That was my prairie dog frame of reference when I moved to Wyoming. Yet again, another animal that does not exist in Massachusetts.

I have a massive bone to pick with Wyomingites. I cannot believe that these playful creatures are considered pests. I could watch them for hours. It's free entertainment.

These whimsical little critters can do no wrong in my eyes, but then again, I'm not a rancher. Still, they are charming.

I can tell you exactly when I saw a pelican in my life, once in Greece and once in Florida. They DO NOT exist in Massachusetts, that I know of, and to be totally honest, I thought they only existed in Florida, in this country anyway. Then I moved to Wyoming (have you noticed a theme yet?). And I can't stop photographing them.

I like to take walks by myself, which I feel completely safe doing here, no matter what time of day, and on one of my walks by the North Platte River, I saw a couple of pelicans. They were floating on the river, presumably looking for a meal, but I like to think they were just being playful, because they would float down river, then fly up river to float down river again. Did I also mention that I love birds? And watching birds do bird things? It's the simple things.

WARNING:

Not only are these photos of a terrible quality, they are pretty graphic.

I thought that these were important to include because they are a major part of my experience here in Wyoming, and from my understanding, it's a very unique experience because not many Wyomingites get to experience this. My husband and I were at Yellowstone National Park, and we decided to get out of the car and walk down a path to see what wildlife we could see because we weren't seeing anything from the road, even though a motorcyclist had told us there was a grizzly bear in the area. We didn't see it.

The cow elk stood by helplessly until she seemingly realized that it was too late.

We set out on this walk, and we heard a screeching noise. I thought maybe it was a bird until I saw a group of cow elk with a calf running out of the trees. The calf was screeching, and it was heart-piercing. Nothing could be done; wolves were chasing them. This is nature.

We were very far away, which is why the picture quality is terrible, so PLEASE NEVER get too close to anything like this. As you can see, the one wolf knew we were there, even though we were about 600 ft. away.

Honorable mentions.
These are just some super cool shots that I got in various places.
I might need a part 2 to this book because it was impossible to include all the photos I have while still keeping this book interesting.

If you have ever seen this sign in Massachusetts, let me know. I never have. But thankfully, I've never seen a rattlesnake either.

The lonely bison bull, probably enjoying the peace and quiet of solitary life, while it lasts.

Just a male mule deer (buck), hanging out in town, nothing to see here.

Some people say that you can see bighorn sheep all over Wyoming. I've seen them once...in Colorado...at Rocky Mountain National Park. Feel free to email me and let me know where they hang out in Wyoming so I can get pictures.

I've been driving for over 20 years, and I received my first speeding ticket in Wyoming.

Ramsay

My domesticated beasties.

Violet

Ozzy

Hugo

Conclusion

By this point, you're probably wondering why I, along with my husband, moved to Wyoming. That is a question that we both get quite often. The simple answer is peace. Peace of mind. Peace in my spirit. Peace in my daily life. Peace in nature. Peace with God. Although there is a more complicated answer, as we are all complicated beings with complicated life experiences, that is the best way for me to convey my answer to you, the reader.

I never felt like I fit in on the East Coast. I always felt like there was more to life than just going to work, coming home, sleeping, and then doing it all over again. I would continually ask God where He wanted me because I felt restless in my spirit. My husband and I discussed it for a while, and I can't say exactly how he felt, but he agreed that he didn't want to live the city life.

I may talk faster than the average Wyomingite, and I may have a weird accent that is hard to understand at times, but at my core, I feel like I belong in Wyoming.

Thank you for reading. I hope you enjoyed this story about a pivotal time in my life. The next time you meet someone from the Bay State, I hope you won't be too quick to judge. We are experiencing this beautiful state and everything in it for the first time. If you were suddenly dropped in the middle of Fall River, Massachusetts, you might feel out of place, too. And like anyone, you'd hope for kindness. That's my hope as well

I also feel that it's important to add that we have met a handful of fellow Bay Staters who now live in Wyoming, and all of us moved here to escape Massachusetts, not to bring it with us.

Random Observations and Things I Miss:

1. The clouds are closer, as I already mentioned.
2. If the clouds are closer, so is the sun. It feels like a laser beam.
3. The weather can be seen for miles. You can spot rain in another county.
4. It's very dry here, which has its positives. In the summer, it doesn't feel like you have a wet towel over your face. But in the winter, my skin feels like sandpaper.
5. One of the most noticeable changes hits you the moment you drive anywhere. There are no tree-lined highways, just plains and mountains that stretch for miles. I've heard that people who visit Massachusetts or another New England state feel claustrophobic because of this, and I get that.
6. When it comes to food, the contrast really stands out. There isn't a lot of variety here.
7. And of course, the accent. Okay, *my* accent. I think people sometimes have a hard time understanding me, probably because I talk a little fast. Or maybe *a lot* fast.

1. I miss the food in Massachusetts. Living 20 minutes from Providence, RI, if we wanted a cuisine that wasn't offered in Fall River, Providence was guaranteed to have it.

And that's it. I miss the food.

www.ingramcontent.com/pod-product-compliance
Lightning Source LLC
Chambersburg PA
CBHW042055090526
44582CB00009B/162